PHOTOS OF PEOPLE AT THE MARCH ON WASHINGTON
AUGUST 28, 1963

TM GIVENS
WITH D. DEAN GIVENS

Pelekinesis

Photos of People at the March on Washington August 28, 1963

by TM Givens and D. Dean Givens

ISBN: 978-1-949790-46-7

Copyright © 2021 TM Givens

Text and Collages by TM Givens

Photography by DD Givens

Layout and book design by Mark Givens

First Pelekinesis Printing 2021

For information: Pelekinesis, 112 Harvard Ave #65, Claremont, CA 91711 USA

Library of Congress Cataloging-in-Publication Data

Names: Givens, D. Dean, 1916-1994, photographer. | Givens, T. M. (Artist),
    author, artist.
Title: Photos of people at the March on Washington, August 28, 1963 / T.M.
    Givens, with D. Dean Givens.
Description: Claremont, CA : Pelekinesis, [2021] | Summary: "Photographs of
    people at the March on Washington, August 28, 1963. Taken by D. Dean
    Givens, these photographs focus on the people gathering at Capitol and
    on the National Mall in preparation for the Civil Rights March. This
    beautiful volume features commentary and observations from artist T.M.
    Givens, the photographer's son"-- Provided by publisher.
Identifiers: LCCN 2021013880 | ISBN 9781949790467 (hardcover)
Subjects: LCSH: March on Washington for Jobs and Freedom (1963 :
    Washington, D.C.)--Pictorial works. | Civil rights
    demonstrations--Washington (D.C.)--History--20th century--Pictorial
    works. | African Americans--Civil rights--History--20th
    century--Pictorial works. | Documentary photography--Washington (D.C.) |
    Washington (D.C.)--History--20th century--Pictorial works.
Classification: LCC F200 .G58 2021 | DDC 975.3/0410222--dc23
LC record available at https://lccn.loc.gov/2021013880

www.pelekinesis.com

to my good friend Henry Jefferson, who encouraged me to know about his own
stories and growing up in Milwaukee, read books by writers about growing up in
a Black World, and find out more than I knew about Black History in America

and

to my publisher Mark whose insight and generosity was/is a great joy. I am
always amazed by his insights and cogent remarks about almost any subject

and

for my one and only guidance through life, Carolyne...
who helps move me through my increasingly slow life.

My dad, Dean Givens, died in 1994. After he died I inherited his photography work, including many of his negatives and prints. I was determined to prepare his photos for publication, as he had hoped to do when he was alive. The main problem was, after I had reviewed them as carefully as I could, I decided that, given the time and work involved with a growing family including a wife and three children, working full time, teaching part time, and the vast combination of prints, contact sheets, frame-able prints and his commentaries, it was not feasible to publish them as he had wished… so, unfortunately they remained idle for some years.

There were about 2,000 prints and/or negatives that were placed in storage after he died in 1994. What you will see in this book are the ones from the 1963 March on Washington that have been sitting in my garage for many years, waiting for me to get organized, or to have some kind of idea about what to do with them.

They focused on his photography of the immense crowd of people arriving and walking throughout the area to where the March was assembling—in front of the White House, on the Park in front of the Capitol, and around the Reflecting Pool. Please understand that I'm writing this on February 2, 2021….a long time after the photos were taken and processed….. Possibly they might be more important after the many current violent uprisings and demonstrations because of the killings of multiple Black people by white city police.

PREFACE

5

REPRODUCTION OF
D. DEAN GIVENS' INTRODUCTION

Our country's interest and concern for the unrest in Viet Nam w[...]
the rise. The riots in the south for equal rights were getting [...]
[di]ctator Castro was waving the flag of communism. Sputnick was cir[...]
[o]ur globe. Martin Luther King, leader of the Equal Rights movement[...]
[a] Dream. A 'march' on Washington was planned for Wednesday, August[...]
1963. The climax of the year came on November 22 in Dallas Texas. [...]
[A] young President Kennedy was assassinated.

During 1962 frequent trips were made from our west coast faci[...]
to the Navy Department. It was early 1963 when a two year duty wa[...]
to the company office on 17th Street. Not far from the office wa[...]
White House and the Mall. Hotel and restaurants were my lifestyl[...]
three weeks. Then feeling secure with the assignment, an apartm[...]
[...] Carillon Apartment building on Wisconsin Ave.,

6

AUGUST 23
A DAY TO REMEMBER
NINETEEN SIXTY THREE

Our country's interest and concern for the unrest in Viet Nam was on the rise. The riots in the south for equal rights were getting vicious. Dictator Castro was waving the flag of communism. Sputnick was circling our globe. Martin Luther King, leader of the Equal Rights movement, Had A Dream. A 'march' on Washington was planned for Wednesday, August 23, 1963. The climax of the year came on November 22 in Dallas Texas. Our young President Kennedy was assassinated.

During 1962 frequent trips were made from our west coast facility to the Navy Department. It was early 1963 when a two year duty was assigned to the company office on 17th Street. Not far from the office was the White House and the Mall. Hotel and restaurants were my lifestyle for three weeks. Then feeling secure with the assignment, an apartment and furniture in the Carillon Apartment building on Wisconsin Ave., N.W. was rented for one year. Arrangements were made for my wife to join me, the apartment was extended to another year.

I routinely rode the bus from the apartment on Wisconsin to the Navy building. It was not uncommon to find protest activities at the north fence of the White House. Viet Nam protesters were not unusual. Some had blankets and food sacks. I knew not which side they were on.

One morning in June, 1963 a march was forming at the White House fence. There was plenty of time to leave the bus with my satchel and camera. It was a protest march to the Department of Justice. The Attorney General, Bobby Kennedy, was the target for declaration of Equal Rights. Most of the marchers were blacks, called 'NEGRO' at that time. Bobby came out on the balcony with a horn to listen and talk.

I was too busy with the camera to tune in on the questions and answers.
After two rolls of film, and an hour, the crowd began to break-up. It was
a good walk back to the main route for a taxi to finish my day at the Navy
building.

I was impressed with the history of the Navy buildings. They were
built when Franklin D. Roosevelt was Under Secretary of the Navy 1913 to
1920. Made of solid reinforced concrete and then forty years old they
had withstood many hardships and renovations.

For weeks and even months before the Freedom March on Washington the
news was filled with riots and troubles in the deep South. I was assigned
a task at the weapons depot in Charleston South Carolina. The news from
the Southern riots was a concern about travel through cities like Charleston.
I was anxious to go and see a friend stationed at the depot. He was a
Commander and in charge of operations. .

The weather was fine as we left our apartment on Wisconsin Avenue
and headed south to Charleston on Interstate-95. It was near noon when
we stopped for lunch at a road house near Fayetteville. This was a treat
in Southern cooking served family style around a table seating eight places.

All was peace and quiet until we arrived in Charleston. As we followed
the map to find our motel, we went through the downtown section of narrow
streets crowded with protest marchers with unkind faces and banners for
equal rights. Not knowing what to expect, or how to act, the windows were
rolled up and a feeble smile glued to our faces.

Almost two months later the news reported a plan for a march on
Washington. Even though there had been little or no violence in the
Washington area I was reluctant to mix in such crowd as we had seen in
Charleston.

8

Both of my cameras use 120 roll film. For most of the scenics AgfaColor, a slide film was used. For something like the Freedom March the Montgomery Ward film ASA 125, available at that time was used. This I could develop and print in a makeshift darkroom in the apartment. There were twenty rolls laid aside for the Freedom March.

By the evening of August 22, 1963 I made the decision to take a bus to the Mall and watch the actions. If it looked favorable I would stay. And-- that it did-- and that I did. Many of the busses arrived the night before. Some had slept on the bus, and some had blankets on the grass. By seven o'clock the action had started, people were moving around-- exploring the area.

The news media were setting up as I made the rounds to find locations for photo opportunities. I wondered if twenty rolls of film would be enough when the action started. Both cameras were loaded with black and white film. With the medium format film of that era there were only twelve shots on a roll.

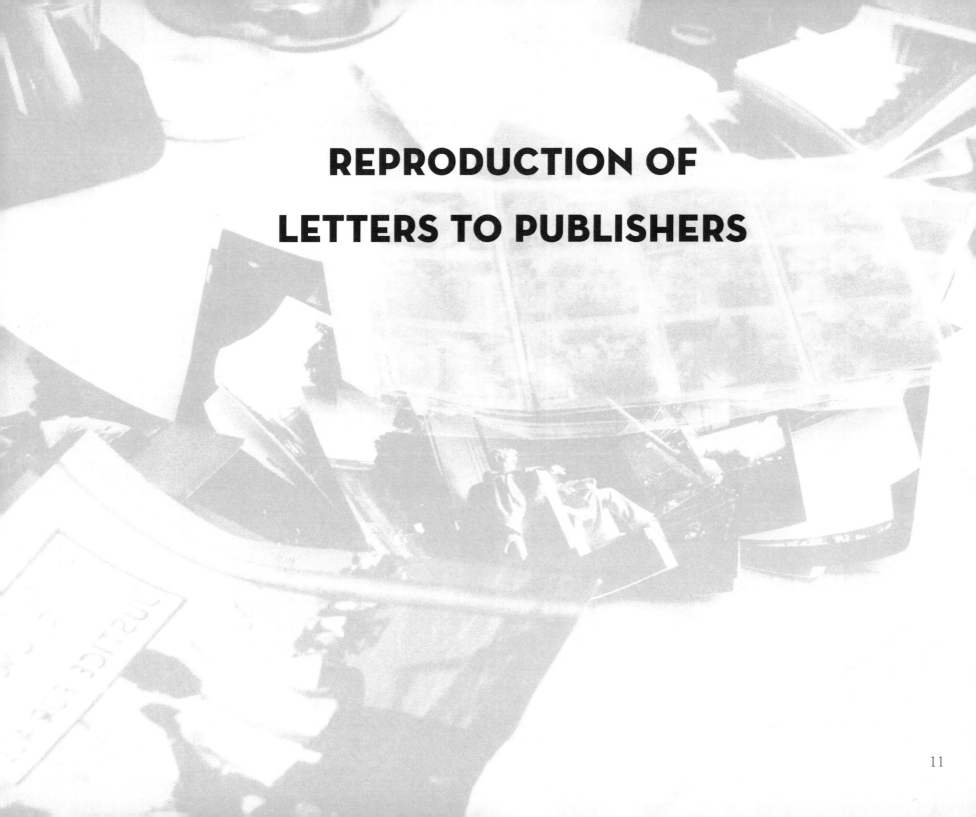

REPRODUCTION OF
LETTERS TO PUBLISHERS

D. DEAN GIVENS
64 RIVIERA, GRANTS PASS, OREGON
97527

File AA

February 20, 1993

SS # 509-07-7977
(503) 471-3665

Query: Publication of picture book of Freedom March
Washington D.C. August 23, 1963, Wednesday.
Simultaneous Submissions

Dear Ms Laing;

The Freedom March could have developed into riots on that Wednesday
of August 23, 1963. The news from the southern states told of fighting
and protest killings. The news of Medger Evers was discouraging. The
forced integration of the white schools created the impression after one
hundred years the 'Civil War' was not over.

The Viet Nam conflict was cause for my several trips to the Navy
Department. In the early spring of 1963 my employer, a west coast aerospace
company, assigned me to their Washington D.C. office.

It was not unusual to see crowds of picketers in front of the White
House. I was never quite sure of their purpose. One morning I left the
bus to watch a crowd headed for the Department of Justice to give Bobby
Kennedy a bad time. I followed along with my camera and brief case. And
was rewarded with some choice pictures of the Attorney General with a bull
horn as he talked and listened for about an hour.

Because of the news of riots and killings in the south I was skeptical
of the Washington Freedom March. But it was a chance in a lifetime. I
caught the earliest bus and found many of the marcher busses had arrived
during the night. Even so, as I wandered around there were many photo
opportunities.

By mid afternoon the speech was over and the crowds were milling around.
In many ways it was like the church picnics we had in our small town in
Western Kansas when I was growing up.
****

My file for the Freedom March contains about 150 well composed and exposed
negatives. The enclosed prints are typical.

I will appreciate assignment for creating the text and photography
for this project.. A prompt response will be appreciated. The market
for such a book should be on the shelves by Martin Luther King's day in
1994. The first two pages of the story are complete and available at your
request.

Enclosures:
    SASE for writer's guide.
    Personal Bio-Summary

Best Regards
D. Dean Givens

12

Q-13

D. DEAN GIVENS
64 RIVIERA, GRANTS PASS, OREGON
97527

File AA

March 30, 1993

SS # 509-07-7977
(503) 471-3665

<u>Query:</u>

Publication
of
A DAY TO REMEMBER
WASHINGTON D.C.
August 23, 1963

5/28/93 Returned w/o Letter.

EDITOR: John Yow
LONGSTREET PRESS INC..
Suite 102, 2150 Newmarket Parkway
Marrieta GA   30067

Same To Wandra & National.

Dear Mr. Yow:

It was thirty years ago this August when the NAACP made great strides
in 'equal rights'. It was special for Dr. Martin Luther King as he delivered
his 'I Have A Dream' speech. My company assigned me to their Washington
office for Navy logistics support which lasted two years. I was privileged
to photograph this on my own time and expense.

The NAACP is the only equal rights organization that has survived
the onslaught of hate and discontent. Now, Benjamin Hook, as Executive
Director is retiring after sixteen years leadership of the organization
which now has over sixty thousand members.

I am in the process of telling the story of that 'peace march'.
With the turmoil throughout the world for equal rights and the physical
practice of 'ethnic cleansing' a coffee table book such as this might be
a good choice.

The enclosed brochures are samples of the design and publication
work I did in the early seventies for the local Chamber of Commerce. The
NAACP photo is one of the options for the cover.

My files include one hundred twenty negatives. The enclosed photographs
are typical of what I plan to use in the story.

****As I progress in the preparation of the text and photographs I will look
forward to working with you on assignment.**

simultaneous submission

ENCLOSURES:
        Photos & Text
Reflecting pool and monument
News wagon
NAACP Marchers
Travel Brochures
        Text Samples
January '93 'A Day'
Abraham Lincoln
Personal Bio-Summary
SASE--Writer's Guide?

REPRODUCTION OF
D. DEAN GIVENS' SUMMARY

pose of freeing the slaves of
thirteenth amendment to the U.S. Constitution abolished slavery
roughout all states.

Equal rights under the and tedious with the
each of those one hundred years. The Socio-political process mo
a snail's pace. society in ge
been slow to accept the black skin as equal to white. Even nov
enlightened decade of the 1990s' there are continuing outward
nonstrations of hate and prejudice.

The 1960s' brought demonstrations and protest in the State Cap
freedom marches throughout the Southern States. Riots and dem
the South brought about the integration of schools, colleges, a
iversities. Prejudice could not be eliminated through the law a
stem, even though 'equal rights' were guaranteed.

The day for Martin Luther King was-- Wednesday, August 23, 1
more than two hundred thousand pilgrims, both black and white g
emselves between the two great monuments of Washington and Linc
celebrate the one hundredth anniversary of the Emancipation Pro
After one hundred years of 'freedom' their rights and privil
d not been fully granted. The political system can go just so
egalize and force, where possible, such rights. It is only throu
dividual of our society, collectively and individually, that f
any group or person is rewarded the privileges guaranteed by t
onstitution. That is the the message of the Freedom March on th
14 1963.

Like the annual pilgrimage to Jerusalem, the March on Washin

****

One hundred thirty years ago the American conscience through Abraham Lincoln recognized what our American Freedom was doing to the black race of people that were hunted in Africa and brought to America as slaves. The slave trade fourished for some two hundred years before 'Honest Abe' issued the Emancipation Proclamation. This document was for the specific purpose of freeing the slaves of the rebellious Southern States. In 1865 the thirteenth amendment to the U.S. Constitution abolished slavery throughout all states.

Equal rights under the law has been slow and tedious with the passing of each of those one hundred years. The Socio-political process moves at a snail's pace. The politics are willing but the society in general has been slow to accept the black skin as equal to white. Even now in our enlightened decade of the 1990s' there are continuing outward demonstrations of hate and prejudice.

The 1960s' brought demonstrations and protest in the State Capitals and freedom marches throughout the Southern States. Riots and demonatrations in the South brought about the integration of schools, colleges, and universities. Prejudice could not be eliminated through the law and legal system, even though 'equal rights' were guaranteed.

The day for Martin Luther King was-- Wednesday, August 23, 1963 as more than two hundred thousand pilgrims, both black and white gathered themselves between the two great monuments of Washington and Lincoln to celebrate the one hundredth anniversary of the Emancipation Proclamation.

After one hundred years of 'freedom' their rights and privileges had not been fully granted. The political system can go just so far to legalize and force, where possible, such rights. It is only through each individual of our society, collectively and individually, that full rights of any group or person is rewarded the privileges guaranteed by the constitution. That is the the message of the Freedom March on this day in 1963.

Like the annual pilgrimage to Jerusalem, the March on Washington has a religious meaning. Many of the church groups carried signs as testimony of their support and belief in the cause of the Great Emancipator. The atmosphere of the group was likened to a great church picnic planned for the nation. The people were friendly, happy and some -very- tired at the end of the day. It was a big event for some who had traveled many miles. Some had traveled so far, and arrived so late, it was time to turn around and go home. Most had sacrificed pay from work time. Some could afford, some could not.

The images recorded in this book show the feeling that prevailed throughout the two hundred thousand marchers. This event was feared by many as a possible explosion into riots. The opposite was true. There seemed to be a calmness of spirit, with an enthusiastic optimism. Violence could serve no productive purpose. There was a great feeling of reverence, perhaps by the proximity to the two great memorials. For many this was a first view of the awesome and magnificent monument to George Washington and the dignified church-like structure that houses the great statue of Lincoln.

As you can perhaps tell, my dad was focused mainly on the technical issues with which he was involved. Not too much about the rationale, purpose, feelings, curiosity, or who was involved about the March itself. He had a different reason to be there.

He was working for the Consolidated Vultee Aircraft Corporation (Convair). His assignment with the company in California had changed and he was sent to Washington D.C. to organize and head the test labs for a specific designated sea-to-air missile. While he was there he also had the time to look at what was occurring in and around D.C. — the variety of protests, demonstrations, and the organization of the March.

I found that there were three sets of photographs he had taken and printed — a set of contact sheets of the negatives themselves, some 4″x 5″ prints which might be enlarged for framing, and some larger prints that he seemed to consider some of his best ones. He had also written a brief paragraph or two for captions at the publication he desired.

As I delved into the collection more deeply, there seemed to be a few distinct sections that could be identified with any purpose or intention that he might have held, so I decided to arrange the prints into five sections, with some text that might add to their purpose or intent.

Contact prints of arrivals and people assembling

Contact prints are the most visible prints of the negative images that were exposed when using black and white film. The examples shown are of folks arriving via busses and moving into the general area of formation. You'll notice that some are dressed in relatively formal clothing because they had arrived to conduct some business of the NAACP while in D.C. and others are dressed in rather casual clothes, which was not unusual because the incoming crowds often stayed in local hotels or residences' homes. For this March on Washington they had come from distant places—as far away as Texas, California and as near as Maryland, Virginia.

Many of the images are of people holding signs and banners from whence they came, organizations and/or what they advocate... NAACP, Baltimore Urban League, Catholic Interracial Council, or signs like "Jobs" or "Kill Jim Crow."

SECTION A

You may notice that red and blue lines are drawn around some images. This is to highlight specific images that Dad might have thought good enough to enlarge (which you will see later.) Many of these images are of people interacting with specific monuments.

You may also notice that there are few photos of major speakers during this March. Dad noted this, even though there is this large photo of AG Kennedy speaking to the crowd a few days prior to the March on August 28, 1963. I think this was not part of Dad's purpose... he didn't know that any of the major speakers would be at the March, so he focused on the people who attended and protested to the U.S. Government. In brief discussions after reviewing some of these photos, Dad's concern was what these folks were up to and why were they protesting. As you may know, this was a summation of the previous sit-ins and conflicts that had occurred primarily in the Southern states prior to the March on Washington. These conflicts—including many lynchings, burnings and sit-ins throughout Alabama, Virginia, Georgia and other Southern States—were part of the call for Negroes to be considered a part of the Human race.

29

Individual Small Prints

These 4"x5" prints are some of the ones selected by Dad for possible enlargement ... those that could be printed as examples of his experiences at the March itself or to illustrate a point that he would make during his unwritten article. Notice that in some of them you can see the immensity of the crowd along the edges of the Reflecting Pool as well as the groups of folks around the collection of recently developed television cameras or at the numerous monuments. Having been in Washington D.C. for only a little time himself, he was amazed at the willing sightseers and some of the print and visual media who were there. As you will also notice, some of these photographs have been enlarged for their graphic image as well.

SECTION B

33

The buildings in the background are those of The Pentagon.

41

Negatives

These images are on the front porch and steps of the Supreme Court on 1st Street NW, behind the U.S. Capitol, showing Attorney General Robert Kennedy speaking to the crowd on a bullhorn. Notice the large television camera on the left side of the photo. This photo was taken shortly after a large meeting of RFK with James Baldwin, Harry Belafonte and Lorraine Hansbury, among others where he heard about ......"what do Negroes want...."*

* Leeming, David Adams, James Baldwin: A Biography, 1995, Henry Holt and Company, 222.

49

Vue·all Neg·Saver
Made in U.S.A.

DATE

TITLE

INSERT FILM EMULSION SIDE DOWN

NO.

Also at this time, the television and other media localization were not identified or marked out. You can see a tv camera in one photo and some tv media doing interviewing in another.

Six collages

These collages were made from photos taken by Dean Givens and organized by me as interpretations that seem to focus on specific topics that might be important. When I say that they "might be important" it is meant to be my interpretation of their meanings, because the images, although caught at different times of the day and in a variety of settings, all seemed to convey similar meanings—the ambiance of the crowds, the gathering of crowds in multiple settings, individuals that were involved in their own activities—designs that incorporate drawing and photography.

AUGUST 28, 1963   MARCH ON WASHINGTON D.C.

COLLAGE BY T.M.GIVENS   DEC.16 2020
PHOTOS BY D.D.GIVENS   AUG.28 1963

The facade and Viet Nam protestors in front of the White House are obvious.

AUGUST 28, 1963   MARCH ON WASHINGTON D.C.

AUGUST 28, 1963   MARCH ON WASHINGTON D.C.

COLLAGE BY T.M. GIVENS   DECEMBER 2020
PHOTOS BY D.D. GIVENS AUGUST 28 1963

YOUTH FELL
UNITED CHI

12/21/20   FROM A PHOTO TAKEN IN 8/28/63
BY D.D. GIVENS

12/16/20 – OK — I've made 3 collages of the Marlin on Washington that Dad took. 2 5x7 & 9 ?x12. Actually, they're pretty good. I think I'll be able to make a few more. maybe frame them for the kids – you know – scan frames – w/ 11x17 frames – maybe do this after Christmas. This Christmas is going to be unusual – maybe Christmas eve w/ them and then have at Thompsons & Greens' – more later, but this going to be a little tougher than before.

I don't think I'd ever grow up – now I'm 82 and I think I'd like to have more kids. I was so fucked up then that I didn't k you what I thought or believed. Think of the guys that were in that class – 2 of them divorced, I disappeared, I suicide and me – pretty sorry! what a sorry group. and I was so screwed up that I went along with 'em. I think about the kids as they were when they were young and what a good time we had. and your much trouble we had –

at the hard times I had with Mark's crying – and the times in the shower with the hot water on – steam – and walking back & forth – what was it? – croup – his breathing. I remember that I felt that I wasn't able to handle it – making the croup tent in listening to him try to sleep... I also think about the times that Krista had the sore hip episode – much too much. She hurt a long time and she kept hurting and I/we couldn't do anything to help her out. was kept hurting and I/we couldn't do anything to help her out. too much! I don't think I'll ever know about how much that hurt her...

12/28/20
Wow, this has been a long time – but I wrote more on other pages... oh well. I thought last night and then all thru the night about my regret over the vasectomy I had – 50 years ago – prob. 1963 – at least after Krista was born what a terrible decision that was – I think we would have had a great time w/ more kids, but I didn't follow C's thoughts about a big family. I was too "controlled" by my "good friends" – the A's & P's. I wanted to be independent, not controlled by "anyone" I think that was the predominant thought of the class back then. but

Single Pages with Multiple Prints

These are some of the direct prints of the negative sheets that contain sections of the films that Dad thought were most memorable. As you page through them, you can see the chronology that he had as he walked through the crowd in front of the Capitol and throughout the park and Reflective Pool.

Some of the images have been cut out by both he and myself—he, because it was a reminder to him for a bigger enlargement and for me, because it was to be part of a collage.

SECTION E

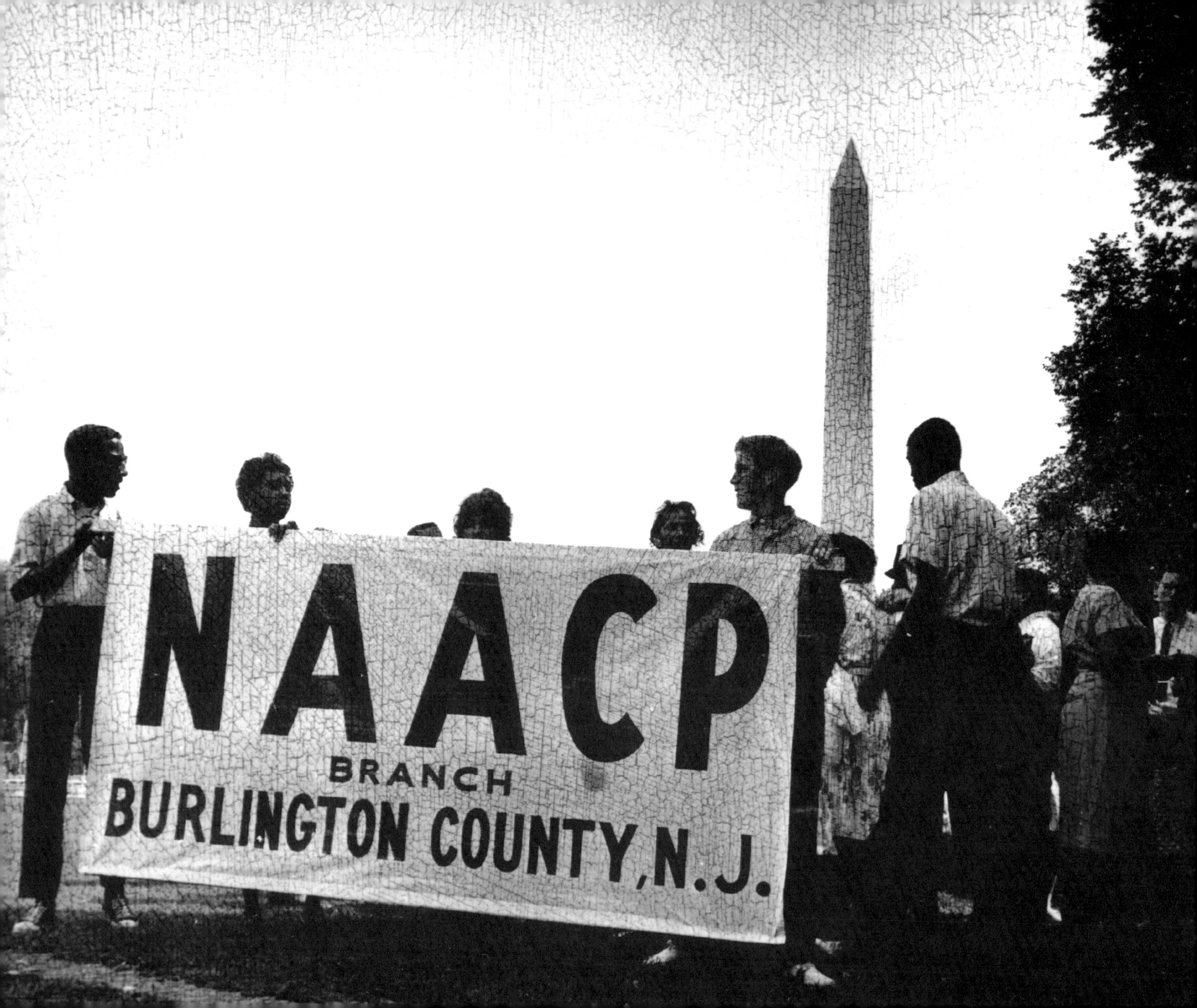
NAACP
BRANCH
BURLINGTON COUNTY, N.J.

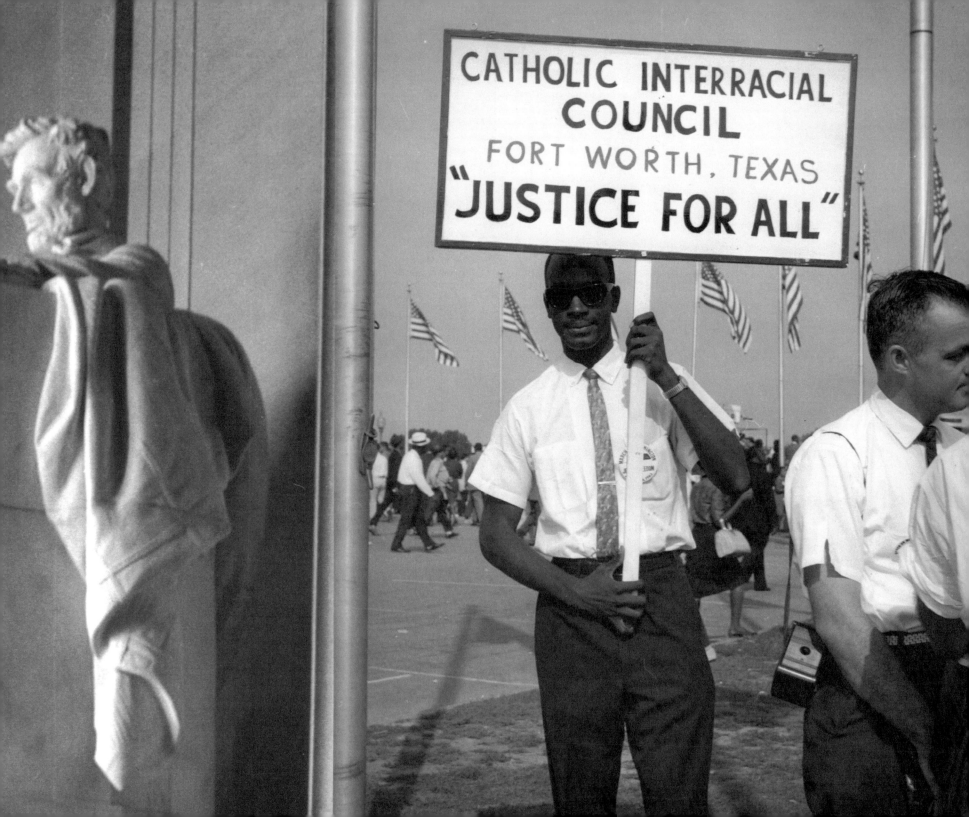

I hope that these photos and the text explain what I intended and what my dad did when he catalogued this momentous journey. He was a curious individual and didn't say too much at home, either about his work or about his feelings or generally about anything that interested him. He was an engineer, totally.

He was born in a small town in Kansas and married my Mom in 1937 and moved to California because of the war and the Navy and then a job offer that built on his Navy-learned skills, as an engineer and thinking process.

His family was comprised of his wife and two kids. We went to Elementary school in San Diego and then to high school in El Monte, California. He worked at a missile plant in Pomona, which is a drivable distance near El Monte. He worked his way up from a draftsman to an administrator of test labs in Pomona and then became involved in multiple projects that involved travels to the Test Labs in the desert and the East Coast (Boston and Washington D.C.)

He became interested and quite a good photographer while I served as a photographer in the Air Force. He had that as his hobby until he retired, when it became his full time vocation. It was also handy when he traveled on his work assignments. His photographs of the March on Washington D.C. were part of his hobby as he neared his retirement.

He was a quiet person, one that did not often show his temper or joys and we did not have many conversations. Basically he was a person who seemed to be a one of the '50s culture—one who did not talk

85

much, was private with most of his friends, and kept his personal life pretty private. Our family was one noted for its spectacular order and friendliness. He was interested in learning as much as he could about the Bible and how its history had an understandable relation to our current activities living in the 1950s and 1960s.

I say this because I don't think that he had much involvement or experience with African-American individuals. As he noted in his written introduction to his photographs, he was just beginning to learn about the NAACP and was interested to know that they were a national organization. So the discovery of his time in Washington D.C. and involvement with the March was kind of unsettling for the rest of us.

I say for the rest of us, primarily because there was not a general discussion with the family about the March or any of the subjects that could have been topics for discussion – slavery, white supremacy, Reconstruction, Civil War, or red-lining.

In fact while they were buying their house in El Monte, I remember that the sales agent mentioned to my dad that El Monte was in a "Sunset" area... which meant that it was illegal for Blacks to be in the city over night. And my parents didn't take any notice about that.

This was much of the attitude during that time in this area of Los Angeles. Not much was discussed about the issues that surrounded us—the riots and violence that occurred in Watts or any of the confrontations that occurred between Hispanics and white sailors. And the newspapers and other news resources, radio and television, did not communicate much about the diversity of the population or conversa-

tions about working together or communication at all.

For my own life, it was only until I was married and near to retirement that I became understanding about these issues that occurred daily or historically in Southern California and our nation. It was a great wake-up call to me and the rest of the family when we learned that he had photographed the March on Washington in 1963 and done a little research about the NAACP. As we talked during the time after both of our parents died, we thought that these forays into the lives and history of African-Americans in our neighborhoods and nation were beginning steps and have been quite an integral history and that none of it had been mentioned or noted in our own personal histories or education.

So, as I began to read, learn, think and talk about this "forgotten history" of our nation, only then did I realize that there was more to do and that Dad had begun something for our family that needed to be continued.

These photographs are the result of that ongoing research and discussion... and my interpretations are of some of his results.

(15)

X

JUN 14 1963

Picktures for Viet Nam
in front of the White
House

JUL 4 1963

(18)

X

JUN 14 1963

(15)

X

JUN 14 1963

(21)

D. DEAN GIVENS
5076 Leonard Rd.
64 Riviera
Grants Pass, OR 97527

© FEB.
1963
© D. Dean Givens

AUG 28 1

AUTHORS

D. Dean Givens in his studio, Oregon, 1981

D.DEAN GIVENS--------64 RIVIERA---------GRANTS PASS,OR.--------97527

BIOGRAPHICAL SUMMARY*********APRIL 27, 1992
NATIVE KANSAN

depression--dustbowl experience
early work--family grocery and butcher shop
permanent marriage since 1936
* one son-one daughter-five grand children*
ONE GREAT GRAND-SON!!!!
* SAFEWAY MARKET MANAGER*--wichita and denver-1937to1943
* ENGINEERING DRAFTSMAN*--major aircraft co.--1943to1945
* NAVY ELECTRONIC SCHOOLS*--honorary discharge--1946
* ELECTRONIC GUIDANCE LAB*--same aircraft co. 1946--as follows
* 1952- SUPERVISE ENGINEERING TEST LAB*
-develop guided missile systems test program-
-develop component quality control test program-
*1957--1960-MOSAIC SUPPLY AND DESIGN SHOP-(wife owned).
-create designs for Italian glass mosaic-
1963- COMPANY OFFICE WASHINGTON D.C.
-navy technical support-
1967-QUINCY SHIPYARD-TEST PROPOSAL
-army fast deployment ship-
1968-FIELD SERVICE POMONA CA DIVISION
-design change contract for navy-
1969-LOGISTICS SUPPORT GROUP
-maintenance analysis-life cycle cost procedures-
1972-EARLY RETIREMENT OPTION
-purchase small motel-O'Brien, Oregon-
-establish and operate photo studio- 18 YEARS
1987-CLOSE STUDIO-SOLD MOTEL
-writing-travel and photography-

PUBLISHED ARTICLES:
*1963-Supervisory Management Magazine: Task Planning
Key to Effective Delegation. Reprint permission to
Thiokol's "Men and Management" Magazine and Conn. Gen.
Life Ins. Co.'s "Notes and Quotes".
* 1971-Machine Design Magazine: Plan Ahead for Product
Maintenance

PHOTOGRAPHIC EVENTS
*1963-Freedom March--Washington D.C.
*1966-Simulated Disaster--New York City
*1969-Handling Procedures, Anti-Radar Missile/A-6 Aircraft
*1975-Hasselblad Merit Award--Black 'n White
*1977-Madame Butterfly-available light
*1979-La Traviata-available light
(operas include publicity in black 'n white)
*1979-Teach Creative Photo course, Rogue Comm. College.
*1981-Aerial Photo Illinois Valley (Oregon)

MORE EDUCATION
*1940-Commercial Art-correspondence course.
*1942-Commercial Art-Denver University (incomplete)
*1963-Certificate-Business Management--U.C.Extension.
*1969-Famous Photographers, Westport Conn. (diploma)
*1982-Color Retouching-Veronica Cass Seminar.
*1983-Airbrush Techniques-Seminar.
*1989-Travel Writing/Photography Seminar (Rogue Com.College.)
***(many special technical and management courses and seminars
during employment.

ENCLOSURE 4

Terry Givens

Terry Givens and his wife Carolyne were married in Claremont, California in 1961. After school and job attempts in San Diego, they returned to Claremont and he finished his education in Art History and Painting at UCR and the Claremont Graduate School.

They have lived in Claremont for the past forty-plus years. He has participated in many Claremont events, namely exhibits at the Claremont Community Foundation and as a featured artist at the Taste of Claremont, sponsored by the Rotary Club of Claremont.

Terry has exhibited in a variety of media, with sculpture at the Ankrum Gallery, the Los Angeles County Museum of Art, Chaffey College, and with drawings and paintings in a variety of galleries in Sacramento. In 2018, the Rancho Santa Ana Botanic Garden exhibited his drawings in a changing exhibition titled "Terry Givens: 100 Garden Views." He has contributed many drawings to organizations, individuals, and businesses in and around Claremont.

In addition, he has curated exhibitions at the Rex Wignall Gallery in Ontario and the Riverside Art Museum.

He taught art and photography in a variety of local elementary and secondary schools, as well as at local universities and colleges.

Terry and Carolyne have three grown, admirable children, four superlative grandchildren and live in Upland.

112 Harvard Ave #65
Claremont, CA 91711 USA

pelekinesis@gmail.com

www.pelekinesis.com

Pelekinesis titles are available through Small Press Distribution, Baker & Taylor, Ingram, Bertrams, and directly from the publisher's website.

CPSIA information can be obtained
at www.ICGtesting.com
Printed in the USA
BVRC100811310821
615688BV00008B/271